ΩΓΧΧ

RINZEN PRESENTS
RMX EXTENDED PLAY

SIDE A
96 RMX

AN EPISODIC COLLABORATION BETWEEN DESIGNERS, ARTISTS & MUSICIANS FROM AROUND THE WORLD, BREATHING LIFE BACK INTO THE DUSTY OLD LUNGS OF EXQUISITE CORPSE.

RINZEN PRESENTS
RMX EXTENDED PLAY

SIDE A
96 RMX

AUSTRALIA, GERMANY, SWITZERLAND, SWEDEN, GERMANY, JAPAN, HONG KONG, USA, UK.

16 WEEKS, 6 THEMES, 96 VISUAL REMIXES, 9 AUDIO REMIXES, 36 PLAYERS, 1 WEEK DEADLINES.

BEND YOUR KNEES ADRIAN CLIFFORD, RINZEN
HAPPY ACCIDENT RILLA ALEXANDER, RINZEN
MAGIC SPRAY POTION KARL MAIER, RINZEN
REPEAT OFFENDER CRAIG REDMAN, RINZEN
SUPER NATIONLIST KATRINA DOBBS, RINZEN
MAYBE LATER STEVE ALEXANDER, RINZEN

INTRODUCTION

RMX EXTENDED PLAY documents a perilous path of visual misadventure through six sequences of reinterpreted themes and contrasting graphic approaches. An episodic collaboration between designers, animators, illustrators and artists from around the world, RMX coaxes breath back into the dusty old lungs of the Exquisite Corpse and repaints his coffin a spritely yellow. A supporting cast of tigers and penguins looks on...

RMX traces its genealogy way back to the year 2000, when the first remixers huddled around campfires, scrawling rough ideograms onto cave walls and clutching their makeshift weapons at each howl of the predatory clients that stalked the cold wastes. Eight of these designers decided to dull the pain of their cro-magnon style existence with a spontaneous swapping of designs – remixing – a collaboration based on surrealist game concepts. The impromptu weekly process quickly developed into something more shapely, organised, and intriguing; the results were collected into a poster pack and web site, and exhibited in Australia and Berlin.

Maintaining the methodology of the first RMX project, EXTENDED PLAY works by pitting each player's ideas and methods of expression against a set of rules and a predetermined thematic phrase for each of the six sequences; apart from that, the rest is in their hands.

One visual piece for each of the six themes of RMX EXTENDED PLAY was produced to begin the project, then passed progressively to each player in sequence, being 'remixed' each step of the way – modified, added to, erased – with each player not seeing the work in progress before their turn commenced.

RMX Best Practice comprised the following rules:

1. Each remix must be completed and returned within one week.
2. Each remix must be produced only with vectors.
3. Remix must not not include any pixel-based elements.
4. Remix must not not include fonts designed by the player.
5. Remix may only include fonts designed by the player.
6. Remix must conform to size and production constraints of the finished book.
7. No player is aware who precedes or follows them and the final pieces will only be revealed at the end of the process.

Once underway RMX EXTENDED PLAY gathered its own momentum (with a few cautious nudges and an inquisitive email here and there) and quickly evolved into the unwieldy, many-hued graphic hydra you are now holding. A testament to the collaborative possibilities offered by email, RMX EXTENDED PLAY spanned the world and allowed participants who might never meet face to face the opportunity to engage in a fleeting but intimate vector relationship. The accelerated deadlines involved also prompted a wide range of approaches to the task – conceptual, loose, mannered, derisive, casual, elaborate, reverential – each piece transfixed by the headlights of the impending weekly handover to the next remixer.

RMX EXTREMELY COMPACT DISC

3 action packed inches of role reversal – for once, a musical project spawned from the seed of a graphic idea, instead of the other way around. Our visual remixers to the RMX project; these sound files were then mangled, manipulated, cut-up, and sequenced into a collection of musical tracks that remix the human voice into something alien and rhythmic – but still oddly familiar.

Conspirators in this accumulation of surgeries operated to the same principal: the only permissible sounds to use in the musical procedure were those generated from the initial voice samples. We gathered together the bloody wrecks and compiled them by methods best left unspoken.

RMX EXTENDED PLAY BONUS ROUND

It has tasted the blood of the fallen, and witnessed struggles both epic and appaling – now it's time to reseed the overworked RMX soil and encourage some virgin growth in our vector-scourged plot of land.

On the RMX EXTENDED PLAY VERY COMPACT DISC you'll find the tools necessary to strap this ox-burden to your creative psyche, and plow on in the name of RMX. The final remix of each RMX EXTENDED PLAY theme sits on the CD in digital format, ready and waiting to be toiled over and dispatched to extendedplay@rmxxx.com in resplendent new forms. Broken and withered, only too late will you realise the truth about The Project That Would Not Die.

Audio remixers too proud and foolish to heed the warning can also indulge – on the disc you'll find the MP3 files you'll need to perform your own audio autopsies and splendid resurrections.

And we're sure we needn't remind you, audio or visual, all remixing needs to follow the established RMX EXTENDED PLAY rules...

Further information is interred at the spiritual resting place of RMX – www.rmxxx.com – where we encourage the idle and unwary to add their own sorry tales to this saga of woe.

Limited Edition
& Bonus Tracks:

AMY FRANCESCHINI FUTUREFARMERS

I am reading a book right now: UTOPIANISM.
H.G. Wells is sighted:
"Our business here is to be Utopian, to make vivid and credible
if we can, first this facet and then that, of an imaginary whole
and happy world. Our deliberate intention is to be not, indeed,
impossible, but most distinctly impracticable, by every scale
that reaches only between today and tomorrow."

That said, I think the RMX Project captures that tension
between possibility and practicability. Urging one to jump
through the fence and fight that battle of restraint or not
wanting to step on someone's toes. Working with the rhythm
of Rilla's encouragement (the theme of the remix), we step
into a movement beyond what lays before us to a place that
will be a stepping stone for someone else to continue on the
yellow brick road...

JASON GROVES SHYNOLA

The results of my remixes are the smoking ruins of a battle
between Illustrator 9.0 and myself. At times I even imagined that
I was winning – what a fool. Let my defeat be a warning to any
unsuspecting fellow Bitmapper...Beware the Vector. I'm returned
home now to lick my wounds and tell horrifying tales of infinite
scaling and bottomless layers. I can see now, the grandchildren
sitting on my knee listening to Pop's tales with their hands over
their eyes and fingers in their ears, revelling in the grisly details.
I just hope that in the modern world we build from the ruins,
there can be peace between us

MATT OWENS VOLUMEONE

Flying blind. Seeing only a small fraction of the whole. Time and energy and work become road blocks. What do I do? How can I find the time? These are questions we all ask ourselves as we create in the digital space. These limitations also serve as the building blocks for creativity. Without constraints, we have nothing to bounce off of, respond to, fall in love with or reject.

The new installment of RMX, featuring designers worldwide, shows what happens when creativity, time and the unknown are placed in front of you and you have to just 'do something'. There is a spirit and energy to RMX that is like no other project. From Switzerland, to Germany to Sweden to Japan to the US – and on – a small visual idea grows and modulates and modifies itself – and individual expression serves as the joystick from which the visual game is played.

These new RMX projects are a breath of fresh air. In each project, you can see the inspiration, the spark of an idea that has gone topsy turvy. These pieces are simultaneously funny and sexy and sheik – equally refined and incomplete – they make you want to create something for fun that makes you laugh. Something you want to share and pin to your wall.

As a mixed up hybrid evolution of creative energies, RMX2 functions not only as a document of a process, but also serves as a snapshot of our creative moment, a moment where creative worlds collide and meld and intertwine. Geography disappears while digital space becomes fluid as ideas and creativity merge into a singular body of work. RMX is a great singular effort and the time and passion of its participants really shows.

EDDIE PAK   THE OFFICE FOR FUN AND PROFIT

The idea of creative collaboration is not new, but it is a relatively modern packaging of the idea that comes to us as "remixing" – the idea that you work off the palette or so-called final product of another creator to create a new result. Obviously, the end results are not without relationships or history. The immediate medium of reference for remixing is music, but now we see this creative process being practiced visually. It takes a bit of loosening of the creative grip to allow for this process to occur, but the result is more spontaneous and the focus does dramatically shift from product to process. Of course, process is one of those things in graphic design that commonly gets put up on a pedestal but in practice gets often overshadowed in the seduction of sexy graphics and latest visual trends.

So with the RMX EXTENDED PLAY project, process really gets put to the test. In some respects, the whole idea behind how this project progresses to the end supersedes the actual graphics – which is obviously not to say the graphics themselves are not engaging. With one consistent theme, the work is passed on from designer to designer after the image is remixed: shuffled around, added to, scaled, drawn upon, etc. There are two types of remix stages. In layman's terms the viewer has the "I see where that came from" stage and the "Where the hell did that come from?" stage.

The viewer can readily see and understand how Tomoko Takeue remixed Adrian Clifford's graphic in Maybe Later; however, it takes a closer observation to understand how Ben Frost remixed Furi Furi's image in Happy Accident. This observation between the remix stages is what is important; noting the comparison from Remix Stage A to Remix Stage B is what the viewer is supposed to understand. By itself, a single image from the whole process loses its place and consequently its full meaning. Stepping back and digesting the whole process, the evidence of remix becomes much more apparent. The same elements persist from step to step, but get altered. Color combinations get passed on, but appear in different places. Ultimately the real focus of the project is inbetween adjacent remixes – what happens from one image to the next.

In idea, the inherent beauty of this project is the fact that there is no end because the process itself is the product. The viewer is not supposed to just look at the last image on the chain. It is about all the images together, and how they (do not) make sense all together. The RMX project is a manifestation of the fresh attitude of reworking that is usually kept to doodles on notepads during client meetings, but brought to an international scale.

NAME	ADRIAN CLIFFORD
COMPANY	RINZEN
NATIONALITY	AUSTRALIAN
LOCATION	AUSTRALIA

RMX EXTENDED PLAY HAS BEGUN...THE INITIAL PIECES ARE
BEING PRODUCED AS WE SPEAK...
THE REST OF THE TIMETABLE IS BEING GRADUALLY
CONFIRMED – IF YOU HAVEN'T GOT BACK TO ME WITH YOUR
PREFERRED DATES PLEASE DO – AND I WILL CONFIRM EACH
ROUND WITH THE PLAYERS AT LEAST A WEEK BEFORE.

NAME   GEORGINA CULLUM
COMPANY   NORTH
NATIONALITY   AUSTRALIAN
LOCATION   AUSTRALIA

JUST A QUICK NOTE TO REMIND YOU OF THE FIRST ROUND OF
REMIXING. EACH OF YOU LUCKY FIRST ROUND REMIXERS WILL
RECEIVE A FILE, TOGETHER WITH THE RULES. THE RESULTING
REMIXES NEED TO BE RETURNED BY THE FOLLOWING SUNDAY.
CAN'T WAIT TO SEE WHAT HAPPENS!

NAME	DICK HANSEN
COMPANY	MIAMY OF SWEDEN
NATIONALITY	SWEDISH
LOCATION	SWEDEN

OKAY, TIME TO REMIX...
THE THEME THAT YOU MUST REMIX TO IS 'BEND YOUR KNEES'.
YOU CAN ADD TO, SUBTRACT FROM AND MODIFY THE EXISTING
ART TO FURTHER COMMUNICATE THIS THEME... BUT YOU
SHOULD NOT DELETE IT ENTIRELY.

ATTAC

KILL DESIGN!
USE EMPTY SPACE FOR POLITICS.
EACH WORD COUNTS.

Association pour une Taxation des Transactions financières pour L'Aide aux Citoyens:

NAME   KATRINA DOBBS
COMPANY   RINZEN
NATIONALITY   AUSTRALIAN
LOCATION   AUSTRALIA

NAME	MATT OWENS
COMPANY	VOLUME ONE
NATIONALITY	TEXAN
LOCATION	USA

I SENT IT....DID YOU GET IT?
UM, NO! MMMM... CAN YOU TRY AGAIN?
I PUT IT IN THE FTP IN A DIRECTORY CALLED MATT. LET ME
KNOW IF YOU GET IT OK.

NAME   RILLA ALEXANDER   ...RUNNING...OUT...OF...TIME...
COMPANY   RINZEN
NATIONALITY   AUSTRALIAN
LOCATION   AUSTRALIA

NAME	ERIK TORSTENSSON
	RAMIRO OBLITAS
COMPANY	WINK
NATIONALITY	SWEDISH
LOCATION	UK

I GOT THE RMX...IT'S BEAUTIFUL...IT ALSO SEEMS TO BE LOCKED IN A WEIRD WAY. IT DOESN'T MATTER HOW MANY TIMES I UNGROUP. HMMM...

COMPANY	TYCOON GRAPHICS
NATIONALITY	JAPANESE
LOCATION	JAPAN

I HAVE ATTACHED THE FILE FOR REMIX PROJECT. IT IS CREATED WITH ILLUSTRATOR 8.0. I ALSO HAVE ATTACHED J-PEG DATA FOR VISUAL SAMPLE. PLEASE LET US KNOW IF THERE ARE ANY PROBLEMS OR QUESTIONS.

NAME   PETER STEMMLER   PLEASE TRY ILLUSTRATOR SOMETIMES.
COMPANY   EBOY   IT'S SOOOO MUCH BETTER !!!!:P
NATIONALITY   GERMAN
LOCATION   USA

NAME   RHYS LEE
COMPANY   NORTH
NATIONALITY   AUSTRALIAN
LOCATION   AUSTRALIA

I'M JUST SENDING ON THE EXACT FILE THAT I GOT BACK...
MAINLY BECAUSE I KNOW YOU USE ILLUSTRATOR SO
HOPEFULLY WHEN YOU OPEN THE FILE IT WILL ALL BE THERE.
THANKS...GOT ALL GOOD...

NAME	LARS EBERLE
	CARSTEN SCHNEIDER
COMPANY	LESS RAIN
NATIONALITY	GERMAN
LOCATION	GERMANY + UK

GLAD TO HEAR THAT YOU LIKED IT. IT REQUIRED A LOT OF DISCIPLINE BECAUSE THE WEATHER IN BERLIN WAS TOO BEAUTIFUL YESTERDAY. EVERYONE ELSE WAS ALLOWED TO BE IN THE BIERGARDENS AND PARKS.

← FOLD HERE

NAME	DIMITRI BRUNI
	MANUEL KREBS
	FABIAN MONOD (ECAL)
COMPANY	NORM
NATIONALITY	SWISS
LOCATION	SWITZERLAND

HALLO,
1.WE GOT THE FILE.
2.WE ARE WORKING ON IT.
3.WE SEND IT TODAY.
4.WE ARE SORRY FOR THE LATE ANSWER.
5.REGARDS.
6.NORM.

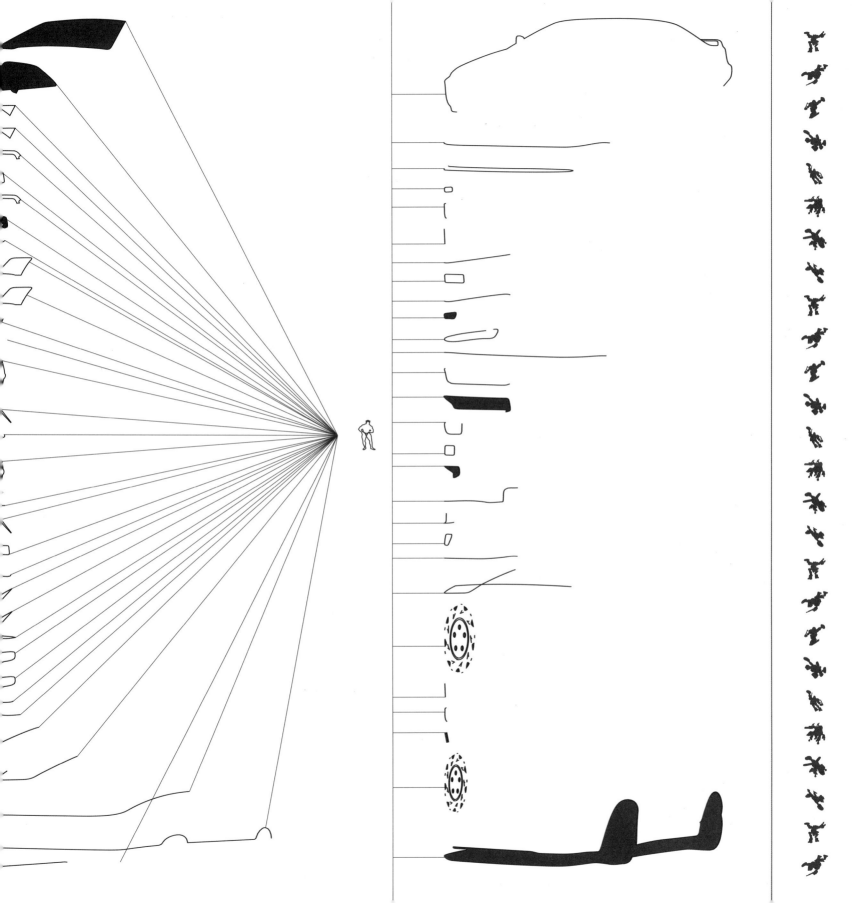

NAME   CHRIS REHBERGER   WHAT A NICE PIECE TO PLAY AROUND WITH...
COMPANY   STANDARD RAD   VERY VERY COOL... IT'S GONNA BE FUN
NATIONALITY   GERMAN
LOCATION   GERMANY

NAME	HENK NIEFELD
COMPANY	SUPERFUN
NATIONALITY	GERMAN
LOCATION	GERMANY

AND HERE IS MY REMIX, IT IS CALLED "KNIEFALL".
DIVERSE IMPORTANT GERMANS IN HISTORY HAVE SIGNED
OR INITIALLED IT...

NAME	RYOSUKE TEI
COMPANY	FURI FURI COMPANY
NATIONALITY	CHINESE
LOCATION	JAPAN

OF COURSE WE ARE READY FOR THE NEXT REMIX!
GIVE US A BIG SHOT!

NAME	EVAN HECOX
NATIONALITY	AMERICAN
LOCATION	USA

I'M BACK, I'VE GOTTEN REALLY BUSY BUT I'M CATCHING UP.
I'LL WORK ON THE REMIX TONIGHT AND SEND IT TO YOU
TONIGHT OR TOMORROW.

NAME   RILLA ALEXANDER
COMPANY   RINZEN
NATIONALITY   AUSTRALIAN
LOCATION   AUSTRALIA

ABOUT THE SOUND...WHAT WE ARE DOING IS AN AUDIO REMIX.
THE BASE MATERIALS ARE THE VOICES OF THE VISUAL
REMIXERS. SO WHAT WE NEED IS A SIMPLE DIGITAL
RECORDING OF SOMEBODY SAYING – IN JAPANESE –
"HALLO WE ARE FURI FURI AND WE ARE REMIXING".
IT ONLY HAS TO BE A COUPLE OF SECONDS LONG.

NAME	RYOSUKE TEI
COMPANY	FURI FURI COMPANY
NATIONALITY	CHINESE
LOCATION	JAPAN

I SEND YOU MY SEXY VOICE...
AND I INTERPRETED YOUR WORK IN A SUPER JAPANESE TASTE.
I ENJOYED RMX WORK. WOW!!!
I AM GLAD IF EVERYBODY LIKE THIS WORK.

MIGHTY GIRL LION PINK

NAME   BEN FROST   HOPEFULLY IT FITS INTO ALL THE RULES.
NATIONALITY   AUSTRALIAN   AND HOPEFULLY IT COMES THRU OK.
LOCATION   AUSTRALIA   YOU MURDERED THE LAST ONE! — BUT HEY, THAT'S THE FUN
                                   OF THE GAME!...

NAME	PETER STEMMLER	...HOW CAN I SEE WHAT COMES OUT !! ?
COMPANY	EBOY	
NATIONALITY	GERMAN	
LOCATION	USA	

NAME	STEFAN GANDL
	BIRTE LUDWIG
	ROB MEEK
COMPANY	DESIGNERSHOCK
NATIONALITY	VARIOUS
LOCATION	GERMANY

I AM A FREEHANDER SO EVERYTHING IS FANTASTIC.

NAME   STEVE ALEXANDER
COMPANY   RINZEN
NATIONALITY   AUSTRALIAN
LOCATION   AUSTRALIA

NAME	HENK NIEFELD
COMPANY	SUPERFUN
NATIONALITY	GERMAN
LOCATION	GERMANY

CAN'T SAY EXACTLY WHAT IT MEANT BUT I DO A LOT OF SPIRIT STUFF LAST TIME...

NAME   KATRINA DOBBS
COMPANY   RINZEN
NATIONALITY   AUSTRALIAN
LOCATION   AUSTRALIA

NAME	DEANNE CHEUK
COMPANY	SURFACEPSEUDOART
	MU
	NEOMU
NATIONALITY	AUSTRALIAN CHINESE
LOCATION	USA

I HOPE THIS IS OK... I WANTED TO SPEND MORE TIME ON IT BUT THERE JUST WASN'T ANY LEFT.

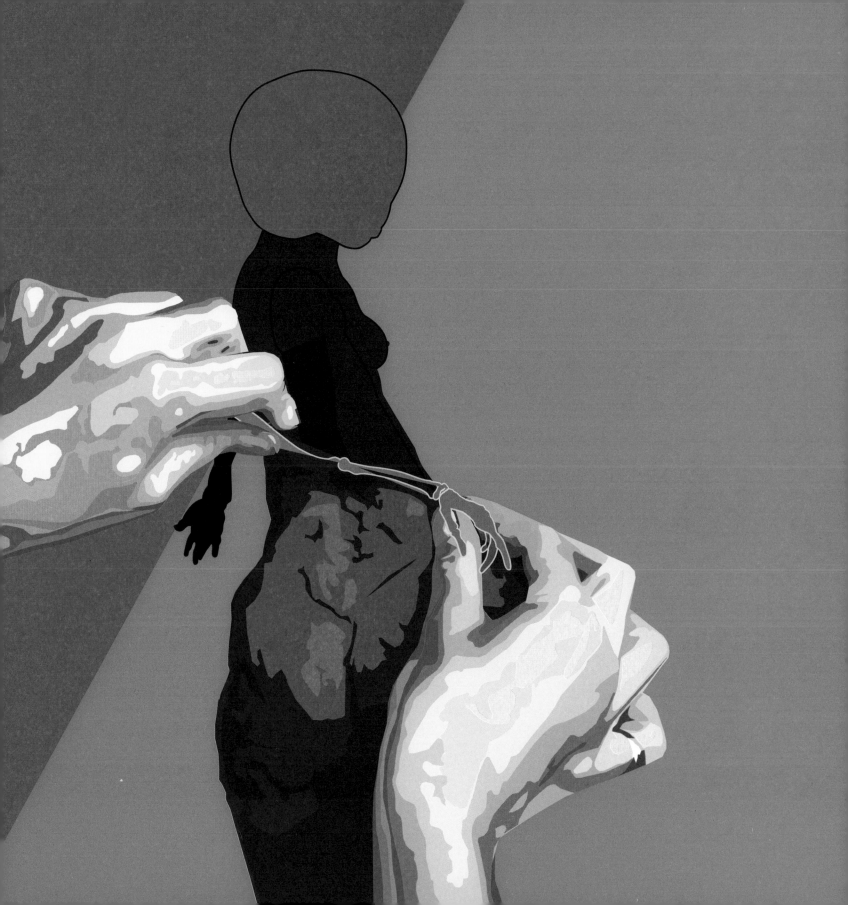

NAME	URS ALTHAUS
COMPANY	HAUSGRAFIK
NATIONALITY	SWISS
LOCATION	SWITZERLAND

HOPE IT'S NOT TOO BIG THE WILDE WHEEL.

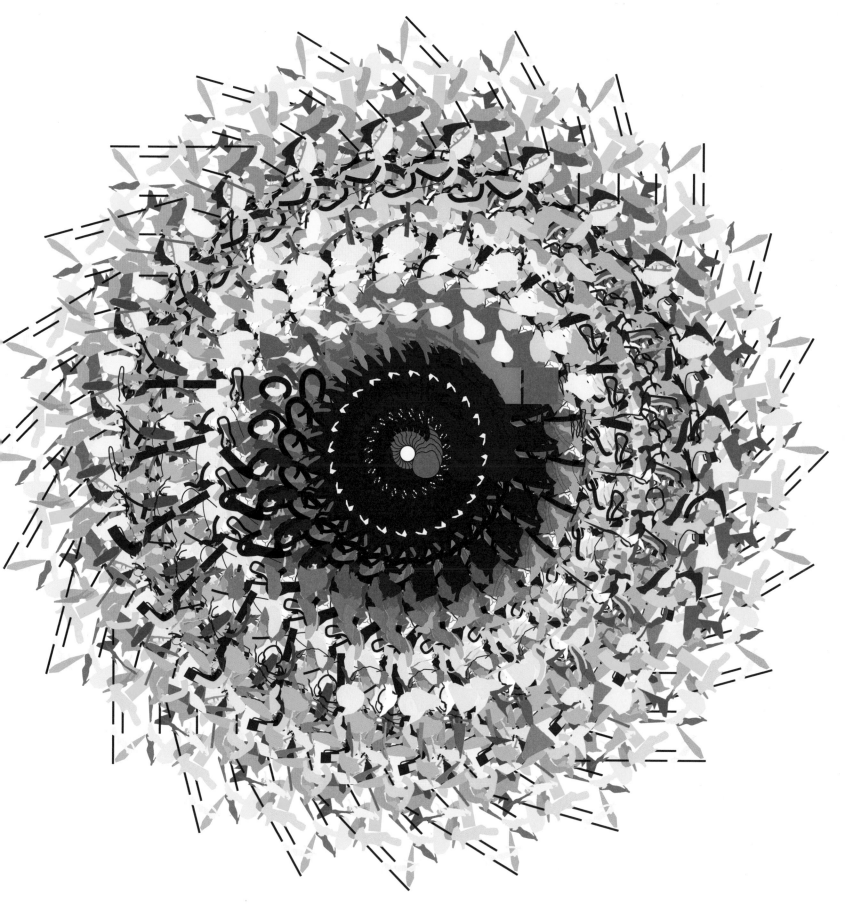

NAME	LARS EBERLE
	CARSTEN SCHNEIDER
COMPANY	LESS RAIN
NATIONALITY	GERMAN
LOCATION	GERMANY + UK

JUST CHECKING WHETHER YOU RECEIVED YOUR LAST REMIX...
AND IF EVERYTHING IS ON TRACK. I NEED TO SEND IT ON AGAIN
ON WEDNESDAY...
WHICH REMIX ARE YOU TALKING ABOUT, DIDN'T YOU RECEIVE
THE STUFF THREE WEEKS AGO?
JUST KIDDING. I NEARLY FINISHED IT YESTERDAY AND WILL
SEND IT OVER WITHIN THE NEXT FEW HOURS.

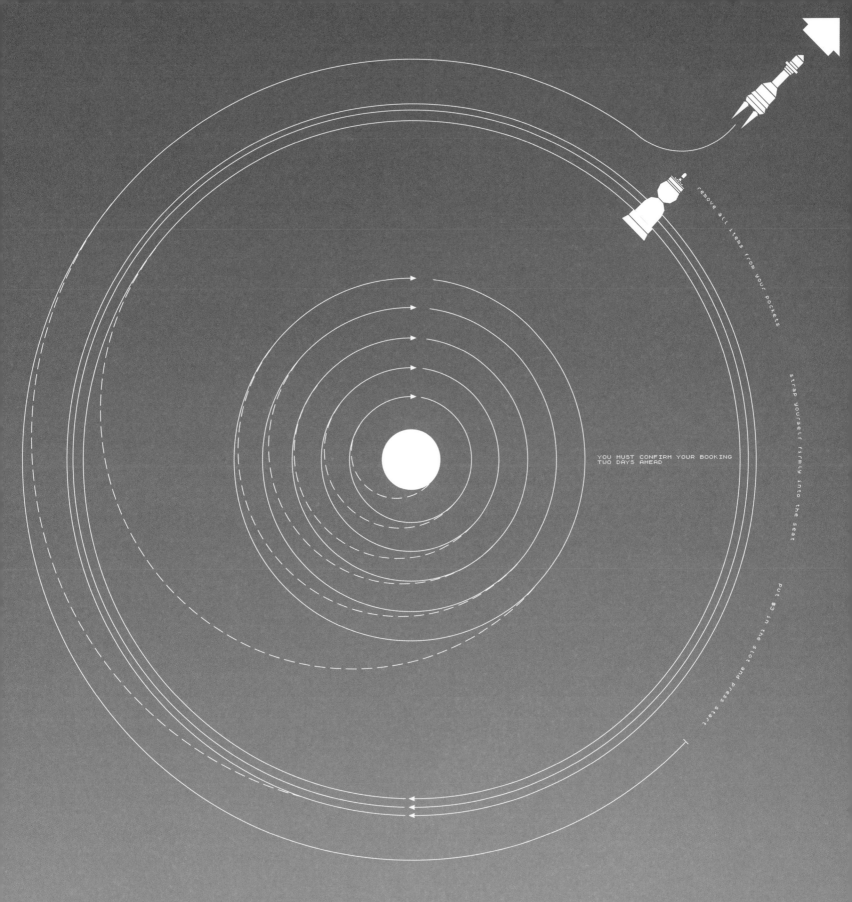

YOU MUST CONFIRM YOUR BOOKING
TWO DAYS AHEAD

remove all items from your pockets

strap yourself firmly into the seat

put yourself into the slot and press start

NAME   MATT OWENS   ALMOST DONE!
COMPANY   VOLUMEONE
NATIONALITY   TEXAN
LOCATION   USA

NAME	DIMITRI BRUNI
	MANUEL KREBS
	FABIAN MONOD (ECAL)
COMPANY	NORM
NATIONALITY	SWISS
LOCATION	SWITZERLAND

THIS IS THE ACCIDENT RMX – CONGRATULATIONS FOR ACE.
THERE WAS THIS HUGE POSTER IN MY BEST FRIENDS ROOM.
I'LL SEND HIM THE DRAWING.

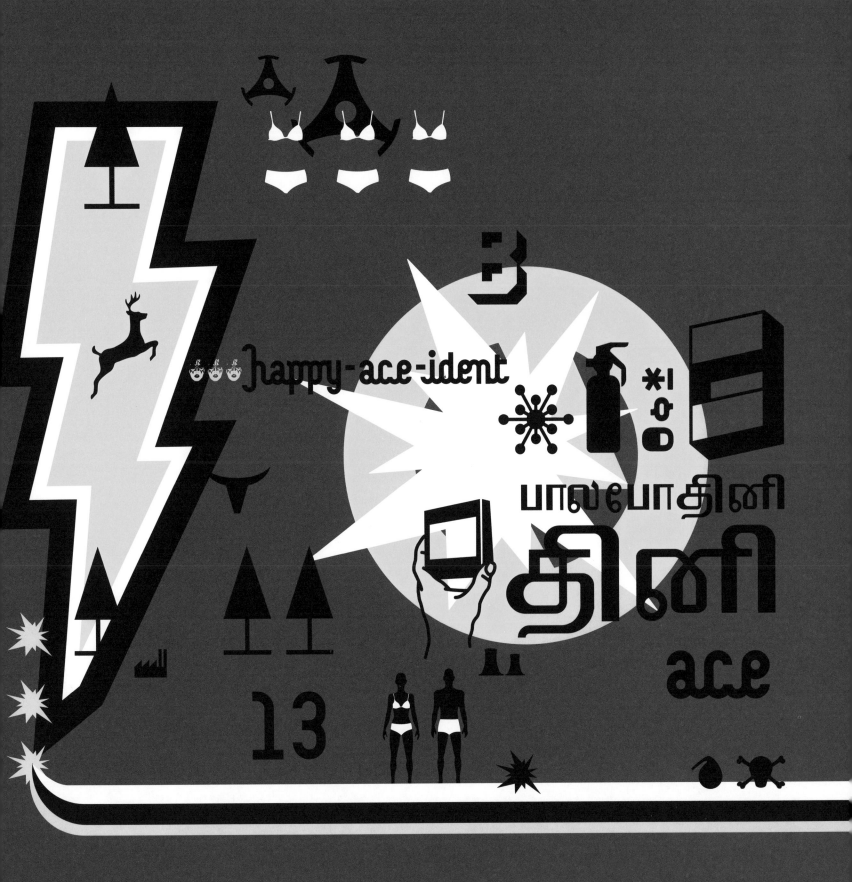

NAME	TOMOKO TAKEUE	
NATIONALITY	JAPANESE	
LOCATION	JAPAN	

DO YOU THINK YOU CAN DO IT THIS WEEK?
YEAH, NO PROBLEM ;)
SEND ME OVER!

NAME   FRANCOIS CHALET
COMPANY   CHALET
NATIONALITY   SWISS
LOCATION   SWITZERLAND

I JUST RECEIVED EVERYTHING BUT I HAD A TERRIBLE STRESS
AND I WILL HAVE FINISHED EVERYTHING FOR YOU MIDDLE OF
NEXT WEEK.

NAME	KARL MAIER
COMPANY	RINZEN
NATIONALITY	AUSTRALIAN
LOCATION	AUSTRALIA

NAME	STEFAN GANDL
	BIRTE LUDWIG
	ROB MEEK
COMPANY	DESIGNERSHOCK
NATIONALITY	VARIOUS
LOCATION	GERMANY

THANKS FOR YOUR MAIL.
GOT EVERYTHING AND LOVE THE PIECE AS WELL.

POPPORNINDUSTRY

XL

POP PORN

MAGIC SPRAY

OH YES! SPRAYED BY DS®   ©06:02:2001   DS® IS A REGISTERED BRAND.

NAME	DEANNE CHEUK
COMPANY	SURFACEPSEUDOART
	MU
	NEOMU
NATIONALITY	AUSTRALIAN CHINESE
LOCATION	USA

G'DAY, THIS IS MY EFFORT!!!
HOPE IT IS UP TO PAR...
I GOT CONFUSED BY THE 'NO 3 DIMENSIONAL IMAGES'.
DID THIS INCLUDE 3D-LIKE IMAGES CREATED IN ILLUSTRATOR?
I DIDN'T DO IT AS I HAD PLANNED JUST IN CASE...

NAME	CRAIG REDMAN
COMPANY	RINZEN
NATIONALITY	AUSTRALIAN
LOCATION	AUSTRALIA

NAME   EDDIE PAK
DAVID YU
THAI NGUYEN
COMPANY   THE OFFICE FOR FUN AND PROFIT
NATIONALITY   AMERICAN
LOCATION   USA

SO, AT WHAT POINT OF THE RMX ARE WE AT RIGHT NOW? WHO
HAS TOUCHED THIS FILE BEFORE? WHO'S GONNA BE WORKING
ON IT AFTER US? JUST INTERESTED AND CURIOUS...

NAME	GEORGINA CALLUM
COMPANY	NORTH
NATIONALITY	AUSTRALIAN
LOCATION	AUSTRALIA

GOT IT! ITS VERY VERY YUMMY.

COMPANY	SWEDEN
NATIONALITY	SWEDISH
LOCATION	SWEDEN

I'LL BE SWIFT AS THE WIND.

NAME	JASON GROVES
COMPANY	SHYNOLA
NATIONALITY	BRITISH
LOCATION	UK

I THINK OUR FINAL PICTURE WILL BE MORE A PRODUCT OF
OUR IGNORANCE WITH VECTORS THAN OUR SENSE OF DESIGN.
(I HOPE YOU LIKE 'NAIVE' ART)

NAME   BEN FROST
NATIONALITY   AUSTRALIAN
LOCATION   AUSTRALIA

I GOT A BIT CAUGHT OUT THIS WEEK, AND DIDN'T MANAGE TO
GET STARTED ON THIS ONE UNTIL SATURDAY.
BUT THAT IS WHAT'S COOL ABOUT RMX, ITS KINDA CAT &
MOUSE, LIKE A SPY MOVIE – TAKING THE MICROFILM TO THE
NEXT LOCATION ETC.

NAME   MAT HINKLEY
NATIONALITY   AUSTRALIAN
LOCATION   AUSTRALIA

ME AGAIN...HERE IT IS AGAIN. I HAVE STILL GIVEN YOU A
STUFFED ONE BECAUSE THE UNSTUFFED ONE IS ABOUT 4MB.
IF THIS DOESN'T WORK THEN I WILL TRY THE UNSTUFFED
VERSION BUT...MIGHT...TAKE...TOO...LONG...

NAME   AMY FRANCESCHINI

COMPANY   FUTUREFARMERS

NATIONALITY   AMERICAN

LOCATION   USA

I'M JUST FINISHING MY REMIX NOW. I'VE BEEN A BAD GIRL AND
BROKEN MY OWN DEADLINE...
WOW. I DID NOT KNOW YOU WERE A FEMALE. I MEAN I DIDN'T
REALLY THINK ABOUT IT, BUT I AM PLEASANTLY SURPRISED!!

NAME   RILLA ALEXANDER
COMPANY   RINZEN
NATIONALITY   AUSTRALIAN
LOCATION   AUSTRALIA

REALLY? THAT'S FUNNY!!!...I WONDER IF YOU WOULD HAVE
FIGURED IT OUT WHEN YOU SAW MY REMIX?

NAME	TOMOKO TAKEUE
NATIONALITY	JAPANESE
LOCATION	JAPAN

HERE IS MY REMIX PIECE! SORRY FOR DELAY... SOMEHOW I COULDN'T SEND ANY EMAILS LAST NIGHT.

COMPANY   EXTRA DESIGN
NATIONALITY   JAPANESE
LOCATION   JAPAN

I TRIED TO AVOID DOING TOO MUCH AS THE FILE IS ALREADY
COMPLICATED ENOUGH.

NAME	DICK HANSEN	CHECKED OUT THE FILE I WAS SUPPOSED TO RMX AND
COMPANY	MIAMY OF SWEDEN	I COULDNT OPEN IT...I'VE UNSTUFFED IT AND TRIED ALL
NATIONALITY	SWEDISH	VERSIONS OF ILLUSTRATOR AND IT WON'T OPEN...
LOCATION	SWEDEN	PLEASE SEND IT AGAIN...

NAME   CRAIG REDMAN
COMPANY   RINZEN
NATIONALITY   AUSTRALIAN
LOCATION   AUSTRALIA

COMPANY	SWEDEN
NATIONALITY	SWEDISH
LOCATION	SWEDEN

HERE'S THE REMIX.
GUARD IT WITH YOUR LIFE.

NAME	DIMITRI BRUNI	
	MANUEL KREBS	
	FABIAN MONOD (ECAL)	
COMPANY	NORM	
NATIONALITY	SWISS	
LOCATION	SWITZERLAND	

THE FILE IS FINE – WE'LL START MIXING RIGHT AWAY –
WE HOPE YOU ARE FINE – IT'S SNOWING IN SWITZERLAND –
BEST WISHES – ? WHEN DO YOU NEED THE FILE BACK ?

NAME	MAT HINKLEY
NATIONALITY	AUSTRALIAN
LOCATION	AUSTRALIA

HORAY HORAY HORAY
THANK YOU THANK YOU THANK YOU
WE HAVE SUCCESS
LANDING CREW DISARM DOORS
CROSSCHECK
WE ARE IN JAMAICA

JAMAICA

COMPANY	TYCOON GRAPHICS
NATIONALITY	JAPANESE
LOCATION	JAPAN

I KNOW IT IS KIND OF LATE TO ASK, BUT WE'D LIKE TO KNOW
THE PRONUNCIATION OF "RMX". IS IT PRONOUNCED AS
"REMIX" OR ALPHABETICAL LETTER "R-M-X"?
PLEASE LET US KNOW.

NAME   DICK HANSEN
COMPANY   MIAMY OF SWEDEN
NATIONALITY   SWEDISH
LOCATION   SWEDEN

JOB IS DONE! TIME TO PASS IT ON TO SOMEONE ELSE...

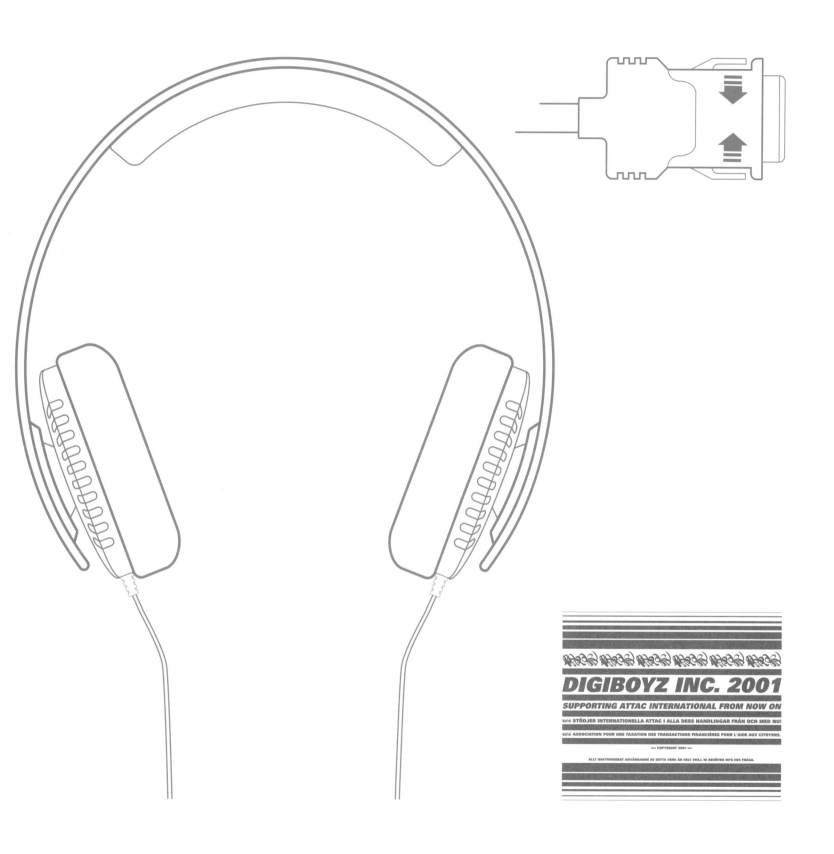

DIGIBOYZ INC. 2001

SUPPORTING ATTAC INTERNATIONAL FROM NOW ON

STÖDJER INTERNATIONELLA ATTAC I ALLA DESS HANDLINGAR FRÅN OCH MED NU!

ASSOCIATION POUR UNE TAXATION DES TRANSACTIONS FINANCIÈRES POUR L'AIDE AUX CITOYENS.

COPYRIGHT 2001

ALLT OAKTORISERAT ANVÄNDANDE AV DETTA VERK ÄR HELT OKEJ. NI BEHÖVER INTE ENS FRÅGA.

NAME   KARL MAIER
COMPANY   RINZEN
NATIONALITY   AUSTRALIAN
LOCATION   AUSTRALIA

repeatoffender

NAME   MATT OWENS
COMPANY   VOLUMEONE
NATIONALITY   TEXAN
LOCATION   USA

NAME	AMY FRANCESCHINI
COMPANY	FUTUREFARMERS
NATIONALITY	AMERICAN
LOCATION	USA

HERE IS A FIRST STREAM OF CONSCIOUSNESS GO AT A REMIX.
I WILL WORK ON IT A BIT MORE, BUT I AM JUST SENDING IT TO
LET YOU KNOW I AM ALIVE AND DO WORK.

NAME   CHRIS REHBERGER
COMPANY   STANDARD RAD
NATIONALITY GERMAN
LOCATION   GERMANY

DEAR OH DEAR... THE LACK OF SLEEP SEEMS TO NEVER GO
AWAY AGAIN WITH YOU. WHAT IS THE MATTER WITH ALL OF US.
I SUPPOSE IT'S CALLED FUN.

GOT THE REPEAT OFFENDER A-OKAY.
IT IS PRETTY, I SEE WHAT I CAN DO.

NAME	EDDIE PAK
	DAVID YU
	THAI NGUYEN
COMPANY	THE OFFICE FOR FUN AND PROFIT
NATIONALITY	AMERICAN
LOCATION	USA

THE OFFICE FOR FUN & PROFIT WILL BE CLOSED FROM FEBRUARY 5TH TO THE 19TH; WE WILL RESPOND TO YOUR EMAIL AS SOON AS POSSIBLE.

NAME	STEFAN GANDL
	BIRTE LUDWIG
	ROB MEEK
COMPANY	DESIGNERSHOCK
NATIONALITY	VARIOUS
LOCATION	GERMANY

EVERYTHING LANDED WELL.

ISBN 3-931126749-1 :N5B1

NAME	ADRIAN CLIFFORD
COMPANY	RINZEN
NATIONALITY	AUSTRALIAN
LOCATION	AUSTRALIA

NAME   PETER STEMMLER   IT'S ALL ABOUT HAVING SEX ON A ROOF IN WILLIEMSBURG,
COMPANY   EBOY   AND LOOKING OVER TO MANHATTAN IN THE PROCESS.
NATIONALITY   GERMAN
LOCATION   USA

NAME	ERIK TORSTENSSON
	RAMIRO OBLITAS
COMPANY	WINK
NATIONALITY	SWEDISH
LOCATION	UK

IT'S ALL READY AND WAITING...THE STUPID SERVER DOESN'T ALLOW E-MAIL OVER 1.5 MB...WHAT TO DO??? DO YOU HAVE ISDN?...PANIC...ADVICE PLEASE...

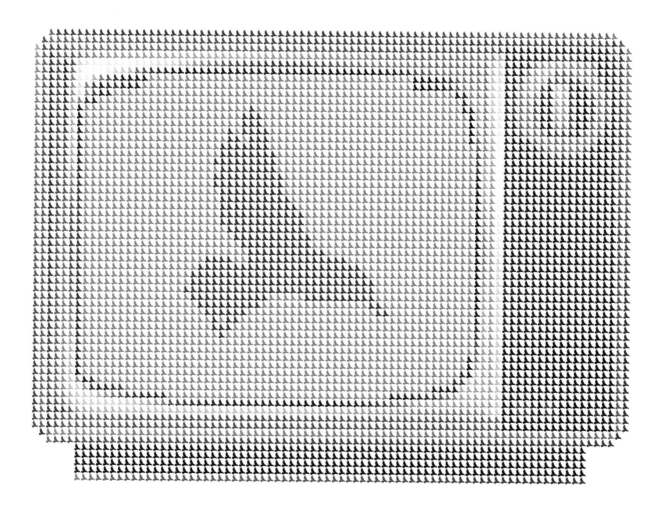

NAME   KATRINA DOBBS
COMPANY   RINZEN
NATIONALITY AUSTRALIAN
LOCATION   AUSTRALIA

NAME   URS ALTHAUS
COMPANY   HAUSGRAFIK
NATIONALITY   SWISS
LOCATION   SWITZERLAND

I'VE RECEIVED THE WORK FROM KATRINA - VERY NICE.
I'M WORKING ON IT.

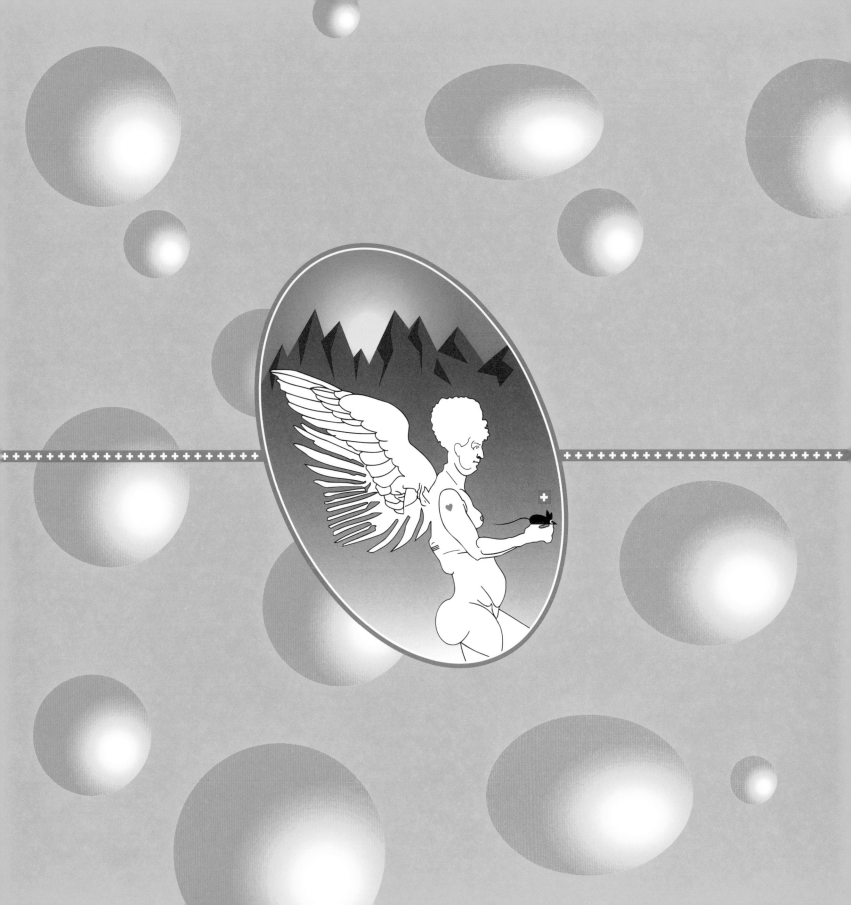

NAME	CHRIS REHBERGER
COMPANY	STANDARD RAD
NATIONALITY	GERMAN
LOCATION	GERMANY

GIMME A BUZZ IF YOU THINK IT'S WAY TOO LITTLE I HAVE LEFT IN THERE...

NAME	ERIK TORSTENSSON
	RAMIRO OBLITAS
COMPANY	WINK
NATIONALITY	SWEDISH
LOCATION	UK

HOW IS THE STUFF YOU HAVE SEEN SO FAR?
IS THERE ANY OTHER SWEDES IN IT?
I'M NOT MEANT TO TELL YOU ANYTHING ABOUT WHAT'S
HAPPENED! ITS A SECRET!!!
OPPSSS...SORRY! SILENCE FROM NOW ON.

NAME	RYOSUKE TEI
COMPANY	FURI FURI COMPANY
NATIONALITY	CHINESE
LOCATION	JAPAN

THIS TOPIC "SUPER NATIONALIST" WAS ALSO VERY INTERESTING. BUT IT WAS ALSO VERY DIFFICULT FOR ME. BECAUSE I'M NOT JAPANESE. BUT I'M VERY SATISFIED WITH THE OUTCOME. I'M VERY EXCITED WHAT THE NEXT ARTIST WILL RMX OUT OF THIS WORK.

NAME	EDDIE PAK
	DAVID YU
	THAI NGUYEN
COMPANY	THE OFFICE FOR FUN AND PROFIT
NATIONALITY	AMERICAN
LOCATION	USA

YEAH, WE'RE FINISHING UP – ALL 3 OF US ARE GOING TO TAKE
TURNS ON TAKING A STAB AT THIS – AS IT COMES BACK TO US.

COMPANY   FILESHARING
NATIONALITY   GERMAN
LOCATION   GERMANY

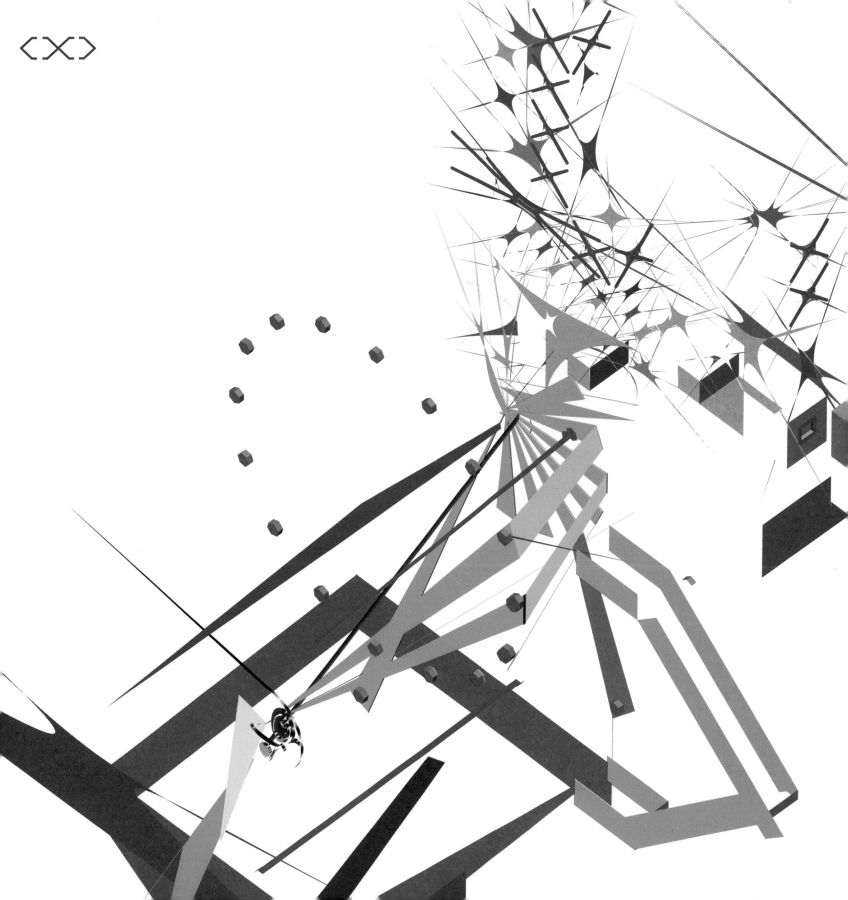

NAME	FRANCOIS CHALET
COMPANY	CHALET
NATIONALITY	SWISS
LOCATION	SWITZERLAND

I SENT IT BACK TO YOU REMIXED LAST FRIDAY.
DIDN'T YOU RECEIVED IT? IF NOT HERE AGAIN.

NAME   EVAN HECOX
NATIONALITY   AMERICAN
LOCATION   USA

* PLEASE NOTE: I'M HAVING DIFFICULTIES WITH MY E-MAIL.
I'M NOT GETTING MAIL WHEN PEOPLE SEND ME A REPLY.
IF YOU NEED TO REPLY, PLEASE START WITH A FRESH E-MAIL
LETTER. HOPEFULLY I'LL HAVE THIS FIXED SOON.

NAME	STEVE ALEXADER
COMPANY	RINZEN
NATIONALITY	AUSTRALIAN
LOCATION	AUSTRALIA

NAME	JASON GROVES
COMPANY	SHYNOLA
NATIONALITY	BRITISH
LOCATION	UK

IT'S NOT THAT I'M LAZY AND DULL WITTED, JUST THAT I'M STRESSED, LAZY AND DULL WITTED. I PROMISE TO BE BETTER BEHAVED NEXT TIME.

COMPANY   SWEDEN
NATIONALITY   SWEDISH
LOCATION   SWEDEN

UUUMM...
GOES SOMETHING LIKE THIS:
NATIONALISM IS A LIE
TOLD TO CREATE UNITY WITHOUT MEANS
AND CONFLICT WITHOUT REASON
PROBABLY A LOUSY TRANSLATION BUT...

NATIONALISMEN ÄR EN LÖGN SAGD ATT SKAPA ENIGHET UTAN MÅL OCH SPLITTRING UTAN MENING

font : firecracker   quote : ⊞ Sweden samhällsinformation

NAME	KARL MAIER
COMPANY	RINZEN
NATIONALITY	AUSTRALIAN
LOCATION	AUSTRALIA

NAME   AMY FRANCESCHINI   I CAN'T WAIT TO SEE THEM ALL IN CONTEXT!!
COMPANY   FUTUREFARMERS
NATIONALITY   AMERICAN
LOCATION   USA

NAME	EXTRA DESIGN
NATIONALITY	JAPANESE
LOCATION	JAPAN

I'M AFRAID THAT EXTRA IS TOO BUSY TO DO THE REMIX IN THE COMING WEEK. CAN WE HAVE BREAK?

NAME   STEVE ALEXANDER
COMPANY   RINZEN
NATIONALITY   AUSTRALIAN
LOCATION   AUSTRALIA

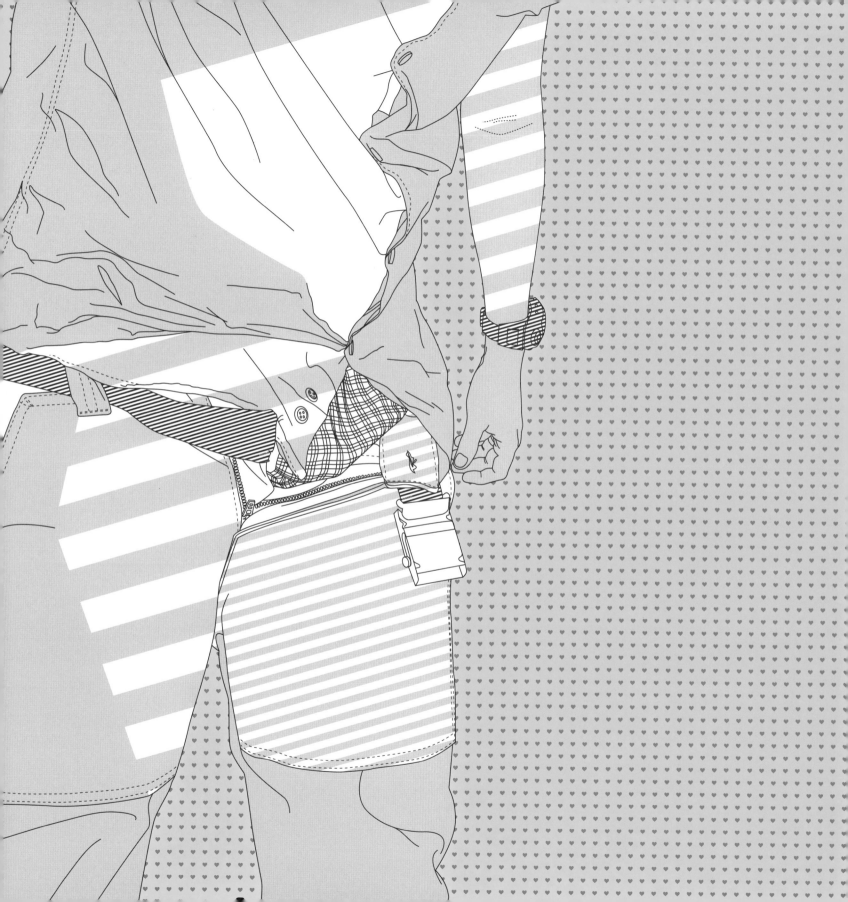

NAME	FRANCOIS CHALET
COMPANY	CHALET
NATIONALITY	SWISS
LOCATION	SWITZERLAND

HAVE A NICE DAY.

NAME   RHYS LEE   SORRY FOR THE DELAY.
COMPANY   NORTH   NO WORRIES! NOW THAT I'VE SEEN IT ALL IS FORGIVEN!!!
NATIONALITY   AUSTRALIAN
LOCATION   AUSTRALIA

NAME	JASON GROVES
COMPANY	SHYNOLA
NATIONALITY	BRITISH
LOCATION	UK

IT SEEMS TO HAVE MYSTERIOUSLY GROWN TO 1.8 MEG SINCE
I STARTED...NOT SURE WHY.

NAME   ADRIAN CLIFFORD
COMPANY   RINZEN
NATIONALITY   AUSTRALIAN
LOCATION   AUSTRALIA

NAME   TOMOKO TAKEUE   SHE'S SOOOO CUTE! BUT YOU KNEW I'D SAY THAT DIDN'T YOU!!!
NATIONALITY   JAPANESE
LOCATION   JAPAN

NAME	BEN FROST
NATIONALITY	AUSTRALIAN
LOCATION	AUSTRALIA

YOU SHOULD DO A 'REAL LIFE' SHOW LIKE SURVIVOR,
BUT WITH AN ALL RMX CAST – WITH IMMUNITY / PRIVILEGE
CHALLENGE – VOTING PEOPLE OUT OF THE GAME AT THE
END OF EACH ROUND, SURVIVAL IN THE HARSH WORLD
OF ART & DESIGN...

NAME	LARS EBERLE	THE FILE SEEMS TO BE FINE SO WE SHOULDN'T HAVE ANY
	CARSTEN SCHNEIDER	PROBLEMS TO START REDESIGNING.
COMPANY	LESS RAIN	MAYBE LATER.
NATIONALITY	GERMAN	
LOCATION	GERMANY + UK	

■ LR R.D.C (RESEARCH AND DEVELOPEMENT COMPLEX)
established 2001 - earlier

many parts of the world still have very limited
access to LR.

world total:0.06

■ LR P.P.C (PROSPECTIVE PRODUCTION CENTRE)
estimated 2002 - later

would-be workers travel abroad under a dual push
and pull effect.

world total:2.44

□ LR P.E.S (PROSPECTIVE EXPANSION SLOT)
estimated 2060 - later

the development of a world economy has accelerated
the destruction of many groups' native homes, but
that does not seem to be eliminating diversity.

world total:89.0

FOR FURTHER INFORMATION, CALL OUR HELPDESK AT
0800 LESS RAIN

S.U.E   P.A.M   M.E.L   I.N.A   K.I.M   L.E.E

please have your ID and personal LR reference
number ready when calling. calls may be monitored
to improve quality of service.

PORT RADIUM

URANIUM CITY

ESKIMO POINT

GOOSE BAY

RENO

LAS VEGAS

LONDON

ALGORTA   MARSEILLES

OMSK

BERLIN

ROME

UPPSALA

SKIATHOS

MURMANSK

TEL AVIV

ULAN BATOR

HONG KONG

NEW YORK

RIO DE JANEIRO
TRINIDAD

KAMCHATKA

YOKOHAMA

MARRAKESH

LAGOS

RIO DE JANEIRO

KATANGA   DAR ES SALAAM

SINGAPORE

SANTIAGO   SANTA FE

MONTEVIDEO

DARWIN

NAME	URS ALTHAUS
COMPANY	HAUSGRAFIK
NATIONALITY	SWISS
LOCATION	SWITZERLAND

BACK IN TOWN AND AFTER ONE AND A HALF DAY
TROUBLESHOOTING WITH MY BIGGEST GUN –
I THINK ALL THE BAD STUFF IS KILLED AND THE HOLIDAYS ARE
STILL WORKING...
I'VE MAKE IT NEW. SOMETIMES PRESSURE OR A BROKEN
PROGRAMME IS NOT THE BADEST WAY TO FIND A NEW AND
MOSTLY BETTER IDEA.

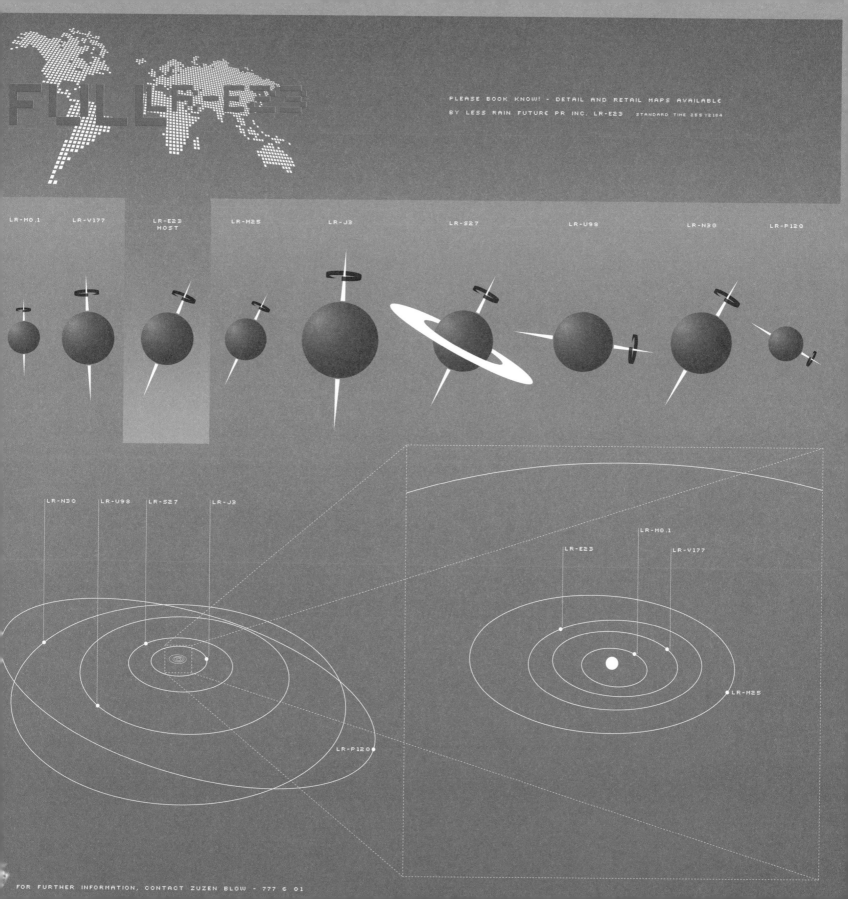

FULL LR-E23

PLEASE BOOK KNOW! - DETAIL AND RETAIL MAPS AVAILABLE
BY LESS RAIN FUTURE PR INC. LR-E23   STANDARD TIME 255 Y2104

LR-M0.1   LR-V177   LR-E23   LR-M25   LR-J3   LR-S27   LR-U98   LR-N30   LR-P120
HOST

LR-N30   LR-U98   LR-S27   LR-J3

LR-E23   LR-M0.1   LR-V177

LR-P120

LR-M25

FOR FURTHER INFORMATION, CONTACT ZUZEN BLOW - 777 6 01

COMPANY   EXTRA DESIGN
NATIONALITY   JAPANESE
LOCATION   JAPAN

HERE'S THE IMAGE.
IS THE RMX PROJECT FINISHED??
NO MORE REMIX FOR US?

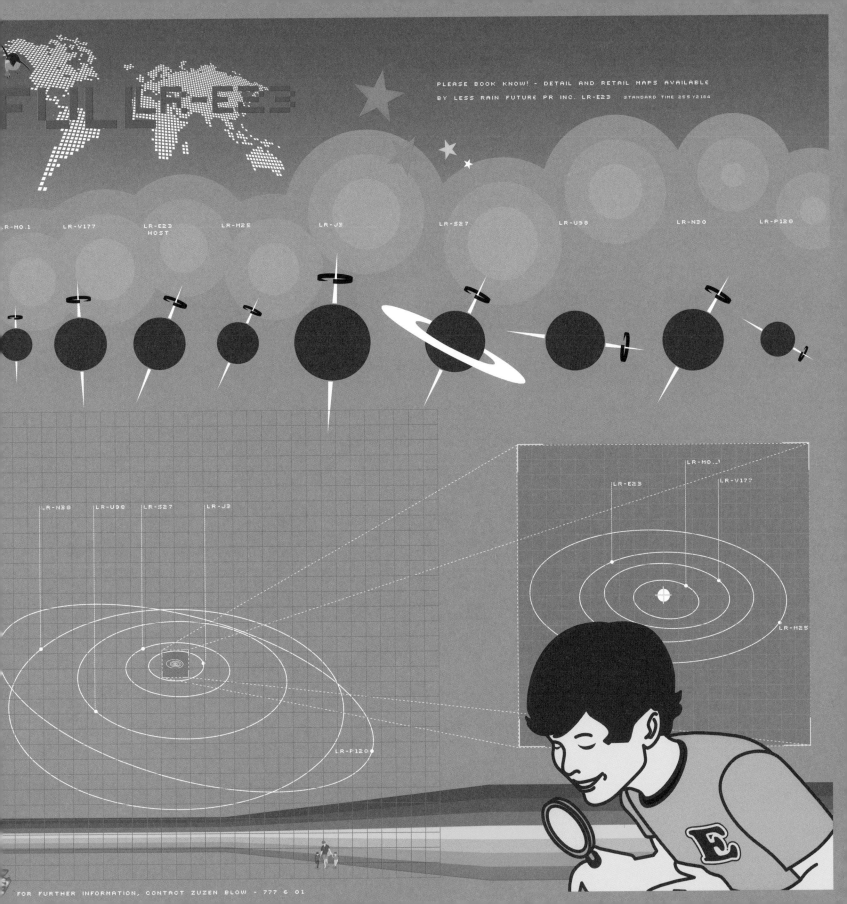

NAME	CRAIG REDMAN
COMPANY	RINZEN
NATIONALITY	AUSTRALIAN
LOCATION	AUSTRALIA

COMPANY
LOCATION

IDN AND SIX STUDIO
HONG KONG

SPECIAL THANKS TO OPTIMUS PRIME.

COMPANY   FILESHARING   FINITO! ;)
NATIONALITY   GERMAN
LOCATION   GERMANY

NAME   MAT HINKLEY
NATIONALITY   AUSTRALIAN
LOCATION   AUSTRALIA

MAT PASSED ME A ZIP LAST NIGHT BEFORE SETTING OFF TO
LONDON ASKING ME TO EMAIL HIS FILE, HERE IT IS, LET ME
KNOW IF IT HASN'T COME THROUGH OKAY.
GOT IT!

COMPANY THE DESIGNERS REPUBLIC HERE YOU GO, THE GRAPHIC IS THE REGISTERED TRADEMARK
LOCATION SOYO/NORTH OF NOWHERE OF THE PHO-KU CORPORATION BY THE WAY.
THAT'S WHAT MAKES IT SO MUCH FUN TO REMIX.

NAME	DEANNE CHEUK
COMPANY	SURFACEPSEUDOART
	MU
	NEOMU
NATIONALITY	AUSTRALIAN CHINESE
LOCATION	USA

I WANT REMIXING TO GO FOREVER!
YAY! ME TOO!

BEND YOUR KNEES

SMOKE AND A SHADOW.

UN, DEUX, THREE.

USE FOR POLITICS.

RIDE ON A HORSE.

A HORSE AND A BUGGY.

ANIMALS AND WHEELS.

BLACK AND WHITE.

RIDE OVER PENGUINS.

HAPPY ACCIDENT

A LITTLE GIRL WAS EATEN BY A LION THAT IS NOW WATCHING MONKEYS AND ELEPHANTS DANCING.

200 YEARS AFTER, SHE BECOMES A LION LADY.

"THIS WAS LAST NIGHT'S DREAM, DAD."
"OK, SON. NOW WHY DON'T YOU TAKE A WALK?"

"WHAT DID YOU DREAM LAST NIGHT?"
"UH... AN EXCITING ACCIDENT... YEAH, THAT WAS AN ACCIDENT!"

AN EXCITING ACCIDENT... MUST BE A CAR ACCIDENT!

I DON'T WANNA DREAM THIS KIND OF ACCIDENT.

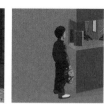

SUPPOSE I'D BETTER READ THE BIBLE BEFORE GOING TO BED.

HMMM...

SEE HER TITS.

THINGS TURNED BLUE.

A CAR AND A MACHO.

FAR FROM HIM.

LIGHT ITS LIGHTS.

DRIVE TO GERMANY.

FART ON THE CAR.

OH MY GOD!

OTHERWISE, I MUST HAVE
A NIGHTMARE.

SOMETIMES THE NIGHTMARE
CAN BE A NAKED WOMAN IF I
RIP THE SKIN OFF.

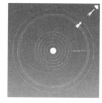

NO! THIS IS NOT THE RIGHT
WAY OF THINKING!
UHHHGGGG.........!!!!!

I DIDN'T MEAN IT,
BUT SOMETIMES SOMETHING
TRIES TO GO OUT, AND IT DID.
THAT'S ALL.

I THINK I JUST NEED A
BIG KISS.

OR A BUNCH OF MY
FAVORITE TOYS.

WHAT!?
DON'T I NEED A GIRLFRIEND?

HELL NO!
DON'T LOOK DOWN ON ME!
I'M A BOY!

MAGIC SPRAY POTION

     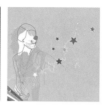

A GIRL JUST SKATED OVER THE SPRAY AND GOT A RAINBOW SHADOW.

DO LOVEDOLLS DREAM OF THE SKATING GIRL? WELL, THEY DON'T BUT SPRAY CANS DO.

THE GIRL DISAPPEARED BUT THE CLOVERS GOT TO THEIR RIGHT POSITIONS.

HERE COMES ANOTHER XXX RATED GIRL WITH SPRAY NIPPLES.

SHE'S NOT TAKING A SHOWER BUT A RAINBOW SPRAY.

YOU CAN SEE THE OTHER SIDE OF HER BY LOOKING AT HER FROM THE OTHER SIDE.

THAT'S ALL THAT I'VE BEEN DREAMING OF, THE SKULL SAYS.

THAT WAS A TERRIBLE WAR, THE SKULL KEEPS SAYING.

REPEAT OFFENDER

YOU USED TO TAKE ME TO THE FIREWORKS EVERY SUMMER, BUT...

WHAT I CAN REMEMBER NOW IS RAIN, CLOUDS AND SOME LIGHT RECOLLECTIONS.

SOMETIMES I REMEMBER THE OUTLINE OF RECOLLECTIONS.

AND SOMETIMES I CAN REMEMBER ONLY SOME PARTICLES...

ONE DAY ON THE VACATION WE WERE AT THE BEACH, AN ASIAN GUY STOLE OUR BAG...

I KNOW YOU DON'T WANT TO HEAR THIS ANY MORE.

I LISTENED TO MY FAVORITE RECORD TILL I GOT SICK OF IT, AND THIS IS WHAT YOU ARE NOW WORRYING ABOUT.

BUT THAT EXPERIENCE GAVE ME AN IDEA TO EARN A BIT OF MONEY.

WHEN LOSING NUMBER OF SOMETHING, WE ALSO HAVE TO THINK OF PRODUCING NEW ONES, DON'T YOU THINK?

IT MUST HAVE BEEN LIKE THIS IF I COULD HAVE EVEN ONE NICE EXPERIENCE.

THINK IT'S ABOUT TIME TO GO. THE TRUCK HAS COME TO PICK ME UP.

UH, GUESS NOT.
THEY FORTUNATELY HAVE COME HERE TO MAKE THE WORLD PEACE. THANKS, MAGIC SPRAY.

SUNSHINE SOMETIMES LOOKS LIKE RAIN.

I LIKE TO SING SONGS IN SUCH WEATHER AS IF I'M DOING WALL-PAINT TO THE AIR.

MAYBE A CLEANING MAN WILL TRY TO WIPE IT OUT.

BUT WHAT HE REALLY NEEDS IS A SPRAY THAT STOPS AND KILLS ANY ATTACKS BY VIRUSES.

I COULD SPEND SWEET DAYS.

SUDDENLY MY LIFE WAS BROKEN EASILY...

I NOW FEEL PAIN AS IF LIONS ARE STARING AT ME.

THAT'S BECAUSE OF YOUR ATTITUDE.

COULD YOU TURN DOWN THE RADIO, PLEASE?

UH...WHAT IS THIS PAIN?
WHO'S FEEDING A DOG WITH MY HEART?

I FEEL AS IF MY CLOTHS ARE ALL TAKEN OFF BY BIRDS.

I WANT TO SHOOT BIRDS AGAIN.

SUPER NATIONALIST

   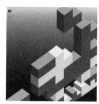   

EVERYTHING STARTS FROM HERE.

THINGS SEEM TO GO THIS WAY.

SOMETIMES THE DARK HORSE RULES.

ONE POSSIBILITY CAN BE THE MAINSTREAM.

THE SUN SMILES TO THE NEW GENERATION.

EVEN THE SUN CAN BE ONE PART OF SOMETHING.

NOTHING CAN KEEP ITS SHAPE FOREVER.

A LIVING THING CAN BE BORN IN CHAOS.

MAYBE LATER

IT'S MORNING NOW AND HE HAS TO GO HOME.

"I'M HOME, HONEY," HE SAYS. OF COURSE, SHE GETS PISSED OFF.

SHE THINKS THAT IT WOULD BE NICE IF HE GETS EATEN BY WILD DOGS.

HE WONDERS IF HE SHOULD MAKE LOVE TO HER RIGHT NOW AS IF THEY ARE WILD DOGS.

HE AND SHE PASS THE BEST JUDGMENT AS ADULTS.

"THIS IS MY MOST FAVORITE PART IN THIS BOOK," A LITTLE GIRL SAYS.

AT THE MOMENT, ANOTHER GIRL IS STANDING ON THE OPPOSITE SIDE OF THE EARTH.

THIS SHOWS HOW THE LAND ON THE EARTH LOOK LIKE.

A LIVING THING CAN EVOLVE AND USE TOOLS TO IDENTIFY ITSELF.

LIVING THINGS CAN GET ORGANIZED TO MAKE A COMMUNITY.

A SUPER HERO WILL BE BORN WHEN PEOPLE'S CONSCIOUSNESS CONCENTRATES.

NOT ALL THE PEOPLE AND COMMUNITIES CAN UNDERSTAND THE DESCRIPTION OF THE HERO.

MISUNDERSTANDING SOMETIMES GIVES A NEW SYMBOL BIRTH.

AN IMPORTED CULTURE TENDS TO MAKE PEOPLE HAVE DIFFERENT POINT OF VIEW FROM THE ORIGINAL.

THE CULTURE CAN BE MADE FROM JUST A SMALL THING.

BY THE PILE OF SMALL THINGS AND BIG THINGS, PEOPLE GET USED TO AND LOVE THE LAND GRADUALLY.

THIS SHOWS HOW THE SOLAR SYSTEM LOOKS LIKE.

THIS SHOWS HOW HAPPY THE BOY IS WHEN HE IS INVESTIGATING THE SOLAR SYSTEM.

THIS SHOWS HOW THE BOY EATS.

THIS SHOWS HOW THE BOY THINKS WHILE EATING.

THE ROBOT THINKS HE MAY BE DECOMPOSED.

SEE.

IS THIS ALL RIGHT OR WRONG?

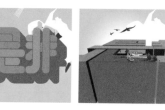

IT TOOK TIME, BUT THE HUSBAND AND THE WIFE GOT THEIR USUAL LIFE AGAIN.

CONCEPT + PROJECT COORDINATION BY
RINZEN

EDITED BY
RILLA ALEXANDER, RINZEN

FOR MORE INFORMATION
WWW.RMXXX.COM

DIE DEUTSCHE BIBLIOTHEK -
CIP EINHEITSAUFNAHME:
RMX EXTENDED PLAY / RILLA ALEXANDER.
HRSG. ROBERT KLANTEN ; HENDRIK HELLIGE.
- BERLIN : DIE-GESTALTEN-VERL., 2001
ISBN 3-931126-74-9

PRINTED BY
MEDIALIS OFFSET, BERLIN

MADE IN EUROPE

FOR YOUR LOCAL DGV DISTRIBUTOR PLEASE
CHECK WWW.DIE-GESTALTEN.DE

REMIXES BY
FRANCOIS CHALET — FRANCOISCHALET.CH
DEANNE CHEUK — NEOMU.COM
DESIGNERSHOCK — DESIGNERSHOCK.COM
PETER STEMMLER, EBOY — EBOY.COM
EXTRA DESIGN — EXTRA.JP.ORG
FILESHARING — FILESHARING.DE
BEN FROST — BENFROST.CJB.NET
FURI FURI COMPANY — FURIFURI.COM
FUTUREFARMERS — FUTUREFARMERS.COM
URS ALTHAUS, HAUSGRAFIK — HAUSGRAFIK.CH
EVAN HECOX — EVANHECOX.COM
MAT HINKLEY — MATHINKLEY76@HOTMAIL.COM
IDN — IDNWORLD.COM
SIX STUDIO — SIXSTUDIO.COM
LESS RAIN — LESSRAIN.COM
MENU|EXIT — UNDERSCAN.DE
DICK HANSEN, MIAMY OF SWEDEN — DICK@NETBABYWORLD.COM
NORM — NORM.TO
RHYS + GEORGE, NORTH — NTHNORTH@BIGPOND.COM
PONY LOAF — DANTEMPLEMAN@HOTMAIL.COM
RINZEN — RINZEN.COM
JASON GROVES, SHYNOLA — SHYNOLA.CO.UK
STANDARD RAD — STANDARDRAD.COM
SUPERFUN — SUPERFUN.NET
SWEDEN — SWEDENGRAPHICS.COM
TOMOKO TAKEUE — TOMOTOMO.NET
THE DESIGNERS REPUBLIC — THEDESIGNERSREPUBLIC.COM
THE OFFICE FOR FUN AND PROFIT — THEOFP.COM
TYCOON GRAPHICS — MAIL@TYG.CO.JP
VOLUMEONE — VOLUMEONE.COM
ERIK + RAMIRO, WINK — WINKMEDIA.COM

WE WISH TO THANK EVERYONE WITHOUT WHOSE ENTHUSIASM AND GENEROSITY WE WOULD NOT HAVE CONCEIVED OF, NOR COMPLETED, THIS PROJECT.

THANKS TO CHRIS REHBERGER, SUPERFUN.5, FILESHARING, BART VAN KERSAVOND, STEFAN GANDL, MATT NAUGHTEN, SK LAM, NEIL THURLOW, RON BOMBELL, RICKI TRTANJ, MATT OWENS AND DEANNE CHEUK.

THANKYOU ALSO TO RALF PYTLIK AND MARK WAGNER OF UNDERSCAN RECORDS FOR MASTERING THE AUDIO.

EXTRA SPECIAL THANKS TO ROBERT KLANTEN AND HENDRIK HELLIGE OF DIE-GESTALTEN VERLAG FOR THEIR TOLERANCE IN THE FACE OF HYSTERIA.

AND OF COURSE, THANKS TO ALL THE REMIXERS FOR PUSHING PAST THE BOUNDARY OF SENSE AND REASON.

RINZEN PRESENTS
RMX EXTENDED PLAY
SIDE B
96 RMX